Bosworth-field: a poem. Written in the year 1629. and dedicated to King Charles I. By Sir John Beaumont, Baronet. With several verses in praise of the author, and elegies on his death, by the greatest wits then living.

John Beaumont

ECCO

PRINT EDITIONS

Bosworth-field: a poem. Written in the year 1629. and dedicated to King Charles I. By Sir John Beaumont, Baronet. With several verses in praise of the author, and elegies on his death, by the greatest wits then living.
Beaumont, John, Sir
ESTCID: T029559
Reproduction from British Library
Also issued as part of: 'A collection of the best English poetry, by several hands', London, 1717.
London : printed and sold by H. Hills, 1710.
39,[1]p. ; 8°

Eighteenth Century
Collections Online
Print Editions

Gale ECCO Print Editions

Relive history with *Eighteenth Century Collections Online*, now available in print for the independent historian and collector. This series includes the most significant English-language and foreign-language works printed in Great Britain during the eighteenth century, and is organized in seven different subject areas including literature and language; medicine, science, and technology; and religion and philosophy. The collection also includes thousands of important works from the Americas.

The eighteenth century has been called "The Age of Enlightenment." It was a period of rapid advance in print culture and publishing, in world exploration, and in the rapid growth of science and technology – all of which had a profound impact on the political and cultural landscape. At the end of the century the American Revolution, French Revolution and Industrial Revolution, perhaps three of the most significant events in modern history, set in motion developments that eventually dominated world political, economic, and social life.

In a groundbreaking effort, Gale initiated a revolution of its own: digitization of epic proportions to preserve these invaluable works in the largest online archive of its kind. Contributions from major world libraries constitute over 175,000 original printed works. Scanned images of the actual pages, rather than transcriptions, recreate the works *as they first appeared.*

Now for the first time, these high-quality digital scans of original works are available via print-on-demand, making them readily accessible to libraries, students, independent scholars, and readers of all ages.

For our initial release we have created seven robust collections to form one the world's most comprehensive catalogs of 18th century works.

Initial Gale ECCO Print Editions collections include:

History and Geography
Rich in titles on English life and social history, this collection spans the world as it was known to eighteenth-century historians and explorers. Titles include a wealth of travel accounts and diaries, histories of nations from throughout the world, and maps and charts of a world that was still being discovered. Students of the War of American Independence will find fascinating accounts from the British side of conflict.

Social Science

Delve into what it was like to live during the eighteenth century by reading the first-hand accounts of everyday people, including city dwellers and farmers, businessmen and bankers, artisans and merchants, artists and their patrons, politicians and their constituents. Original texts make the American, French, and Industrial revolutions vividly contemporary.

Medicine, Science and Technology

Medical theory and practice of the 1700s developed rapidly, as is evidenced by the extensive collection, which includes descriptions of diseases, their conditions, and treatments. Books on science and technology, agriculture, military technology, natural philosophy, even cookbooks, are all contained here.

Literature and Language

Western literary study flows out of eighteenth-century works by Alexander Pope, Daniel Defoe, Henry Fielding, Frances Burney, Denis Diderot, Johann Gottfried Herder, Johann Wolfgang von Goethe, and others. Experience the birth of the modern novel, or compare the development of language using dictionaries and grammar discourses.

Religion and Philosophy

The Age of Enlightenment profoundly enriched religious and philosophical understanding and continues to influence present-day thinking. Works collected here include masterpieces by David Hume, Immanuel Kant, and Jean-Jacques Rousseau, as well as religious sermons and moral debates on the issues of the day, such as the slave trade. The Age of Reason saw conflict between Protestantism and Catholicism transformed into one between faith and logic -- a debate that continues in the twenty-first century.

Law and Reference

This collection reveals the history of English common law and Empire law in a vastly changing world of British expansion. Dominating the legal field is the *Commentaries of the Law of England* by Sir William Blackstone, which first appeared in 1765. Reference works such as almanacs and catalogues continue to educate us by revealing the day-to-day workings of society.

Fine Arts

The eighteenth-century fascination with Greek and Roman antiquity followed the systematic excavation of the ruins at Pompeii and Herculaneum in southern Italy; and after 1750 a neoclassical style dominated all artistic fields. The titles here trace developments in mostly English-language works on painting, sculpture, architecture, music, theater, and other disciplines. Instructional works on musical instruments, catalogs of art objects, comic operas, and more are also included.

The BiblioLife Network

This project was made possible in part by the BiblioLife Network (BLN), a project aimed at addressing some of the huge challenges facing book preservationists around the world. The BLN includes libraries, library networks, archives, subject matter experts, online communities and library service providers. We believe every book ever published should be available as a high-quality print reproduction; printed on-demand anywhere in the world. This insures the ongoing accessibility of the content and helps generate sustainable revenue for the libraries and organizations that work to preserve these important materials.

The following book is in the "public domain" and represents an authentic reproduction of the text as printed by the original publisher. While we have attempted to accurately maintain the integrity of the original work, there are sometimes problems with the original work or the micro-film from which the books were digitized. This can result in minor errors in reproduction. Possible imperfections include missing and blurred pages, poor pictures, markings and other reproduction issues beyond our control. Because this work is culturally important, we have made it available as part of our commitment to protecting, preserving, and promoting the world's literature.

GUIDE TO FOLD-OUTS MAPS and OVERSIZED IMAGES

The book you are reading was digitized from microfilm captured over the past thirty to forty years. Years after the creation of the original microfilm, the book was converted to digital files and made available in an online database.

In an online database, page images do not need to conform to the size restrictions found in a printed book. When converting these images back into a printed bound book, the page sizes are standardized in ways that maintain the detail of the original. For large images, such as fold-out maps, the original page image is split into two or more pages

Guidelines used to determine how to split the page image follows:

• Some images are split vertically; large images require vertical and horizontal splits.
• For horizontal splits, the content is split left to right.
• For vertical splits, the content is split from top to bottom.
• For both vertical and horizontal splits, the image is processed from top left to bottom right.

Bosworth-Field:

A
POEM.

Written in the Year 1629 and Dedicated
to King *CHARLES* I.

By Sir *JOHN BEAUMONT*, Baronet.

With several VERSES in Praise of the Author,
and ELEGIES on his Death, by the greatest
Wits then living.

LONDON:
Printed and Sold by *H. Hills* in *Black-fryars*
near the Water-side, 1710.

TO THE
King's most Excellent Majesty.

Most Gracious Sovereign,

I Here present at the Feet of your Sacred Majesty these Orphan Verses, whose Author (had he survived) might have made this Gift somewhat more correspondent to so Great a Patron. I have only endeavoured without Art, to set this Jewel, and render it apt for your Majesty's Acceptance; to which Boldness I am led by a Filial Duty in performing the Will of my Father, who, whilst he lived, did ever intend to your Majesty this Poem: A Poem, in which no obscene Sport can be found (the contrary being too frequent a Crime among Poets,) while these (if not too bold I speak) will challenge your Majesty for their Patron, since it is most convenient, that the purest of Poems should be directed to you, the Vertuosest and most Untouch'd of Princes, the Delight of *Bri-*

tain,

tain, and the Wonder of *Europe* ; at the Altar of whofe Judgment, bright erected Flames, not troubled Fumes, dare approach. To your Majefty muft be directed the moft precious Off-fprings of each Mufe, which though they may well be efteemed Stars, yet how can they fubfift without the Afpect of you their Sun? Receive then, Great King, thefe my Father's Verfes, and let them find, (what his Son hath found) your Princely Clemency. Effect on them (I befeech your Majefty) a Kingly Work, give them Life, and withal gracioufly pleafe to accept the fincere Wifhes for your Felicity, and the humble Vows of

your Majefty's ever

Loyal Subject,

John Beaumont.

An ELEGY *to the Living Memory of his Deceafed Friend,* Sir John Beaumont, *Knight, Baronet.*

TO tell the World what it hath loft in thee,
    Were but in vain; for fuch as cannot fee,
Would not be griev'd to hear, the Morning Light
Should never more fucceed the gloomy Night.
Such only whom thy Vertue made, or found
Worthy to know thee, can receive this Wound:
Of thefe each Man will duly pay his Tears
To thy great Memory, and when he hears
One fam'd for Vertue, he will fay, So bleft,
So good his *Beaumont* was, and weep the reft.
If Knowledge fhall be mention'd, or the Arts,
Soon will he reckon up thy better Parts:
At naming of the Mufes, he will ftreight
Tell of thy Works, where fharp and high Conceit,
Cloath'd in fweet Verfe, give thee immortal Fame,
Whilft Ignorance doth fcorn a Poet's Name.
And then fhall his Imagination ftrive,
To keep thy grateful Memory alive,
By Poems of his own; for that might be,
Had he no Mufe by force of knowing thee.
This maketh me (who in the Mufes Quire
Sing but a Mean) thus boldly to afpire,
To pay fad Duties to thy honour'd Herfe,
With my unpolifh'd Lines, and ruder Verfe.

Yet

Yet dream I not of raiſing amongſt Men
A laſting Fame to thee by my frail Pen :
But rather hope, ſomething may live of me,
(Perhaps this Paper) having mention'd thee.

THOMAS NEVILL.

An ELEGY *dedicated to the Memory of
his much Honoured Friend, Sir* John
Beaumont, *Knight and Baronet.*

I Write not Elegies, nor tune my Verſe,
  To wait in Mourning Notes upon thy Herſe
For vain Applauſe, or with deſire to rank
My ſlender Muſe 'mongſt thoſe, who on the Bank
Of *Aganippe's* Stream can better ſing,
And to their words more ſenſe of Sorrow bring.
That ſtirs my Genius, which ſhould excite
Thoſe pow'rful Wits : To do a pious Right
To Noble Vertue, and by Verſe convey
Truth to Poſterity, and ſhew the way
By ſtrong Example, how in Mortal State
We Heav'nly Worth may love, and imitate.
Nay, 'twere a great Injuſtice, not to ſave
Him from the Ruins of a ſilent Grave,
Who others from their Aſhes ſought to raiſe,
To wear (given from his hand) Eternal Bays.
It is by all confeſs'd, thy happy Strains,
  Diſtill'd from Milky Streams of Native Veins,

Did

Did like the living fource of *Nafo's* Song,
Flow to the Ear, thence gently glide along
Down to the Heart, in Notes fo Heav'nly fweet,
That there the Sifter-Graces feem'd to meet,
And make thy Breaft their State for foft retire,
And place from whence they fetch'd *Promethean*
To kindle other Hearts with pureft Flame　(Fire,
Of modeft Verfe, and unaffected Fame:
While pedant Poetafters of this Age,
(Who ftile their faucy Rhimes, Poetick Rage)
Loofe Humours vent, and Ballad-Line extrude,
Which grieve the Wife, captive the Multitude.
And that thy Poem might the better take,
Not with vain Sound, or for the Author's fake,
Which often is by fervile Spirits try'd,
Whilft Heav'n-bred Souls are left unfatisfy'd;
Like to the Bee, thou didft thofe Flow'rs felect,
That moft the tafteful Palate might affect,
With pious Relifhes of things Divine,
And difcompofed Senfe with Peace combine.
Which (in thy *Crown of Thorns*) we may difcern,
Fram'd as a Model for the beft to learn:
That Verfe may Vertue teach, as well as Profe,
And Minds with Native Force to Good difpofe,
Devotion ftir, and quicken cold Defires,
To entertain the warmth of Holy Fires.
There may we fee thy Soul exfpaciate,
And with true Fervour fweetly meditate
Upon our Saviour's Sufferings; that while
Thou feek'ft his painful Torments to beguile,
With well-tun'd Accents of thy zealous Song,
Breath'd from a Soul transfix'd; a Paffion ftrong,

We better Knowledge of his Woes attain,
Fall into Tears with thee, and then again,
Rife with thy Verſe to celebrate the Flood
Of thoſe Eternal Torrents of his Blood.
Nor leſs Delight (Things ſerious ſet apart)
Thy ſportive Poem yields with heedful Art
Compoſed ſo, to miniſter Content,
That though we there think only Wit is meant,
We quickly by a happy Error, find
In cloudy Words, clear Lamps to light the Mind.
Then bleſs that Muſe, which by untrodden ways
Purſuing Vertue, meets deſerved Bays
To crown it ſelf, and wandring Souls reduce
From Paths of Ignorance, and Wits abuſe;
And may the beſt of *Engliſh* Laureats ſtrive,
Thus, their own Fun'ral Aſhes to ſurvive.

THOMAS HAWKINS.

To the Worthy Muſe of his Noble Friend,
Sir John Beaumont, *Knight, Baronet.*

WE do not uſher forth thy Verſe with theſe,
That thine may by our Praiſe the better
pleaſe:
That were impertinent, and we too weak,
To add a Grace, where ev'ry Line doth ſpeak,
And ſweetly eecho out in this rich ſtore,
All we can any way pretend, and more.

Yet

Yet since we stand engag'd, we this make known,
Thy Lays are unaffected: Free; Thine own;
Thy Periods, Clear; Expressions, Genuine,
Muse most Emphatical; and Wit, Divine.

THOMAS HAWKINS.

A Congratulation to the Muses, for the immortalizing of his dear Father, by the Sacred Vertue of Poetry.

YE Heav'nly Sisters, by whose sacred Skill,
    Sweet Sounds are rais'd upon the forked Hill
Of high *Parnassus:* You, whose tuned Strings
Can cause the Birds to stay their nimble Wings,
And silently admire: Before whose Feet,
The Lambs, as fearless, with the Lions meet.
You, who the Harp of *Orpheus* so inspir'd,
That from the *Stygian* Lake he safe retir'd;
You could *Amphion's* Harp with Vertue fill,
That even the Stones were pliant to his Will.
To you, you therefore I my Verse direct,
From whom such Beams Celestial can reflect
On that dear Author of my Life inspir'd
With Heavenly Heat, and Sacred Fury fir'd;
Whose Vigour, quench'd by Death, you now revive,
And in this Book conserve him still alive.
Here lives his better part, here shines that Flame,
Which lights the Entrance to Eternal Fame.

These

These are his Triumphs over Death, this Spring
From *Aganippe*'s Fountains he could bring
Clear from all Drofs, through pure Intentions
   drain'd,
His Draughts no fenfual Waters ever ftain'd.
Behold, he doth on every Paper ftrow
The Loyal Thoughts he did his Sov'reign owe.
Here reft Affections to each neareft Friend,
And pious Sighs, which noble Thoughts attend;
Parnaffus him contains, plac'd in the Quire
With Poets: what then can we more defire
To have of him? Perhaps an empty Voice,
While him we wrong with our contentlefs Choice,
To you I this attribute, Sifters Nine;
For only you can caufe this Work Divine;
By none but you could thefe bright Fires be found;
Prometheus is not from the Rock unbound,
No *Æfculapius* ftill remains on Earth,
To give *Hippolitus* a fecond Birth.
Since then fuch God-like Pow'rs in you remain,
To work thefe Wonders, let fome Soul contain
His Spirit of fweet Mufick, and infufe
Into fome other Breaft his fparkling Mufe.
But you perhaps, that all your Pow'r may fpeak:
Will chufe to work on Subjects dull and weak:
Chufe me, infpire my frozen Breaft with Heat,
No Deed you ever wrought, can feem more great.

                    JOHN BEAUMONT,

                                  Upon

Upon the following Poem *of my dear Father, Sir* John Beaumont, *Baronet, deceased.*

YOU, who prepare to read grave *Beaumont*'s
    Verse,
And at your Entrance view my lowly Strains,
Expect no flatt'ring Praises to rehearse
The rare Perfections, which this Book contains.
   But only here in these few Lines, behold
The Debt which I unto a Parent owe;
Who, though I cannot his true Worth unfold,
May yet at least a due Affection show.
   For should I strive to deck the Vertues high,
Which in this Poem (like fair Gems) appear;
I might as well add Brightness to the Sky,
Or with new Splendour make the Sun more clear.
   Since ev'ry Line is with such Beauties grac'd,
That nothing farther can their Praises found:
And that dear Name which on the Front is plac'd,
Declares what Ornaments within are found.
That Name, I say, in whom the Muses meet,
And with such Heat his Noble Spirit raise,
That Kings admire his Verse, whilst at his Feet,
Orpheus his Harp, and *Phœbus* casts his Bays.
   Whom, though fierce Death hath taken from our
    Sights,
And caus'd that curious Hand to write no more;
Yet marvel not if from the Fun'ral Rites
Proceed these Branches never seen before.

For

For from the Corn arife not fruitful Ears,
Except at firft the Earth receive the fame:
Nor thofe rich Odours which *Arabia* bears,
Send forth fweet Smells, unlefs confum'd with
    Flame.
  So from the Afhes of this Phœnix flie
Thefe Off fprings, which with fuch frefh Glory
    fhine;
That whilft time runneth he fhall never die,
But ftill be honour'd in this famous Shrine:
  To which, this Verfe alone I humbly give;
  He was before: but now begins to live.

FRANCIS BEAUMONT.

Upon the Poem of his deareft Brother, Sir John Beaumont, *Baronet.*

WHEN Lines are drawn greater than Na-
    ture, Art
Commands the Object, and the Eye to part,
Bids them to keep at diftance, know their place,
Where to receive, and where to give their Grace;
I am too near thee, *Beaumont*, to define
Which of thofe Lineaments is moft Divine,
And to ftand farther off from thee, I chufe
In filence rather to applaud thy Mufe,
And lofe my Cenfure; 'tis enough for me
To joy, my Pen was taught to move by thee.

GEORGE FORTESCUE.

On the Honour'd Poem *of his Honoured Friend, Sir* John Beaumont, *Baronet,*

THIS Book will live; It hath a *Genius* : This
    Above his Reader, or his Praiſer, is.
Hence, then, prophane : Here needs no words ex-
    pence
  In Bulwarks, Rav'lins, Ramparts, for Defence,
Such, as the creeping Pioneers uſe
  When they do ſweat to fortifie a Muſe.
Though I confeſs a *Beaumont*'s Book to be
  The Bound, and Frontier of our Poetry;
And doth deſerve all Monuments of Praiſe,
  That Art, or Engine, on the Strength can raiſe.
Yet, who dares offer a Redoubt to rear ?
  To cut a Dike ? or ſtick a Stake up, here,
Before this Work ? where Envy hath not caſt
  A Trench againſt it, nor a Batt'ry plac't ?
Stay, till ſhe make her vain Approaches. Then
  If maimed, ſhe come off, 'Tis not of Men
This Fort of ſo impregnable acceſs,
  But higher Power, as ſpight could not make leſs,
Nor Flatt'ry ! but ſecur'd, by the Author's Name,
  Defies, what croſs to Piety, or good Fame.
And like a hallow'd Temple, free from taint
  Of Ethniciſm, makes his Muſe a Saint.

BEN. JOHNSON.

To

To the dear Remembrance of his Noble Friend, Sir John Beaumont, Baronet.

THIS *Posthumus*, from the Brave Parents Name,
  Likely to be the Heir of so much Fame,
Can have at all no Portion by my Praise:
Only this poor Branch of my with'ring Bays
I offer to it, and am very glad,
I yet have this; which if I better had,
My Love should build an A'tar, and thereon
Should offer up such Wreaths as long agon,
Those daring *Grecians*, and proud *Romans* crown'd;
Giving that Honour to their most Renown'd.

  But that brave World is past, and we are light,
After those glorious Days, into the Night
Of these base Times, which not one Hero have,
Only an empty Title, which the Grave
Shall soon devour; whence it no more shall found,
Which never got up higher than the Ground.

  Thy Care for that which was not worth thy Breath,
Brought on too soon thy much lamented Death.
But Heav'n was kind, and would not let thee see
The Plagues that must upon this Nation be,
By whom the Muses have neglected been,
Which shall add Weight and Measure to their Sin;
And have already had this Curse from us,
That in their Pride they should grow barbarous.

  There is no Splendor, that our Pens can give
By our most labour'd Lines, can make thee live
Like to thine own, which able is to raise
So lasting Pillars to prop up thy Praise,
As time shall hardly shake, until it shall
Ruine those things, that with it self must fall.

MI. DRAYTON.

Ad Posthumum opus D. *Jo. Bello-montij,* Equitis aurati & Baronetti, viri Nobilissimi,

HENDECASYLLABON.

Lectum *discubui; biceps gemello*
  Parnassus *bijugo imminebat: unde*
Fontes desiliunt leves, loquaces;
Pellucent vitreo liquore fontes.
Sudo sub Jove, *sydere & secundo*
Discumbo.   *Teneras rosas pererro*
Narcissum, *Violas odore gratas,*
Unguento Ambrosio *has & has refectas.*
Quas inter Philomela *cantitillat*
Præpes, blandula, mellilinguis ales.
Quas inter volitant Apollinesque,
Et Musæ Veneresque mille, mille.
  Insomne hoc sibi somnium quid audet?
Altùm effare noema Bello-montis :
Effatum euge! Poëma Bello-montî *est*
Dîum, castalium nitens, politum;
Libatum salibus, lepore tinctum.
Decurrens velut amnis alti-monte
Feruet delicijs, ruit profundo
Beaumontus *latice.*   *Altiùs resultat*
Fertur, nec tenui nec visitatâ
Pennâ per liquidam ætheram, biformis.
Hic Phœbi *Deus est, decus cohortis*
Summum Palladiæ, *jubar sororum,*
Ipse & flos Venerum, *resurgo; legi.*

PH. KIN.

Upon the *Honoured Poem of his Unknown Friend, Sir* John Beaumont, *Baronet.*

I Knew thee not, I speak it to my Shame:
But by that clear, and equal Voice of Fame,
Which (with the Sun's bright Course) did joyntly
  bear
Thy Glorious Name, about each Hemisphere.
Whiles I who had confin'd my self to dwell
Within the strait Bounds of an obscure Cell,
Took in those pleasing Beams Wit and Worth,
Which, where the Sun could never shine, break
  forth :
Wherewith I did refresh my weaker Sight,
When others bath'd themselves in thy full Light.
But when the dismal Rumour was once spread,
That struck all-knowing Souls, of *Beaumont* dead :
About thy best Friends 'twas my Benefit,
To know thee only by thy living Wit ;
And whereas others might their Loss deplore,
Thou liv'st to me just as thou didst before.
In all that we can value Great, or Good,
Which were not in these Cloaths of Flesh and Blood,
Thou now hast laid aside, but in that mind,
That only by it self could be confin'd,
Thou liv'st to me, and shalt for ever reign,
In both the Issues of thy Blood and Brain.

JA. C4.

Bosworth.

Bosworth-Field:

A

POEM.

THE Winters Storm of Civil War I sing,
    Whose End is crown'd with our Eternal Spring,
Where Roses joyn'd, their Colours mix in one,
And Armies fight no more for *England*'s Throne.
Thou Gracious Lord, direct my feeble Pen,
Who (from the Actions of ambitious Men,)
Hast by thy Goodness drawn our joyful Good,
And made sweet Flowers, and Olives grow from Blood,
While we delighted with this fair Release,
May climb *Parnassus*, in the Days of Peace.

The King (whose Eyes were never fully clos'd,
Whose Mind opprest, with fearful Dreams suppos'd,
That he in Blood had wallow'd all the Night)
Leaps from his restless Bed, before the Light :
Accursed *Tirell* is the first he spies,
Whom threatning with his Dagger, thus he cries;
" How dar'st thou, Villain, to disturb my Sleep,
" Were not the smother'd Children buried deep ?
" And hath the Ground again been ript by thee,
" That I their rotten Carkases might see ?
The Wretch astonisht, hastes away to slide,
(As damned Ghosts themselves in Darkness hide)

And calls up three, whose Counsels could aſſwage
The ſudden Swellings of the Prince's Rage:
Ambitious *Lovell*, who to gain his Grace,
Had ſtain'd the Honour of his Noble Race:
Perfidious *Cateſby*, by whoſe curious Skill,
The Law was taught to ſpeak his Maſter's Will:
And *Ratcliffe*, deeply learn'd in courtly Art,
Who beſt could ſearch into his Sovereign's Heart;
Affrighted *Richard* labours to relate
His hideous Dreams, as ſigns of hapleſs Fate:
" Alas! *(ſaid they)* ſuch Fictions Children Fear,
" Theſe are not Terrors, ſhewing Danger near,
" But Motives ſent by ſome propitious Power,
" To make you watchful at this early Hour;
" Theſe prove that your victorious Care prevents
" Your ſlothful Foes, that ſlumber in their Tents,
" This precious time muſt not in vain be ſpent,
" Which God (your Help) by Heav'nly means hath lent.
He (by theſe falſe Conjectures) much appeas'd,
Contemning Fancies, which his Mind diſeas'd,
Replies: " I ſhould have been aſham'd to tell
" Fond Dreams to wiſe Men: whether Heav'n or Hell,
" Or troubled Nature theſe Effects hath wrought:
" I know, this Day requires another Thought,
" If ſome reſiſtleſs Strength my Cauſe ſhould croſs,
" Fear will increaſe, and not redeem the Loſs;
" All Dangers clouded with the Miſt of Fear,
" Seem great far off, but leſſen coming near.
" Away, ye black Illuſions of the Night,
" If ye combin'd with Fortune, have the Might
" To hinder my Deſigns: ye ſhall not bar
" My Courage ſeeking glorious Death in War.
Thus being chear'd, he calls aloud for Arms,
And bids that all ſhould riſe, whom *Morpheus* charms.
" Bring me *(ſaith he)* the Harneſs that I wore
" At *Teuxbury*, which from that Day no more
" Hath felt the Batt'ries of a civil Strife,
" Nor ſtood between Deſtruction and my Life.

Upon

Upon his Breaft-plate he beholds a Dint,
Which in that Field young *Edward's* Sword did print:
This ftirs Remembrance of his heinous Guilt,
When he that Prince's Blood fo fouly fpilt.
Now fully arm'd, he takes his Helmet bright,
Which like a twinkling Star, with trembling Light
Sends radiant Luftre through the darkfome Air ;
This Mask will make his wrinkled Vifage fair.
But when his Head is cover'd with the Steel,
He tells his Servants, that his Temples feel
Deep piercing Stings, which breed unufual Pains,
And of the heavy Burden much complains.
Some mark his words, as Tokens fram'd t' exprefs
The fharp Conclufion of a fad Succefs.
Then going forth, and finding in his way
A Soldier of the Watch, who fleeping lay ;
Enrag'd to fee the Wretch neglect his part,
He ftrikes a Sword into his trembling Heart,
The hand of Death, and Iron Dulnefs takes
Thofe leaden Eyes, which nat'ral Eafe forfakes :
The King this Morning Sacrifice commends,
And for Example, thus the Fact defends ;
I leave him as I found him, fit to keep
The filent Doors of everlafting Sleep;

Still *Richmond* flept: For Worldly Care and Fear
Have times of paufing, when the Soul is clear,
While Heav'n's Director, whofe Revengeful Brow
Would to the guilty Head no reft allow;
Looks on the other part with milder Eyes :
At his Command an Angel fwiftly flies
From facred Truth's perfpicuous Gate, to bring
A cryftal Vifion on his Golden Wing.
This Lord thus fleeping, thought he faw and knew
His Lamb-like Uncle, whom that Tyger flew,
Whofe powerful words encourage him to fight :
' Go on juft Scourge of Murder, Vertues light,

' The

' The Combat, which thou shalt this Day endure,
' Makes *England*'s Peace for many Ages sure,
' Thy strong Invasion cannot be withstood,
' The Earth assists thee with the Cry of Blood,
' The Heav'n shall bless thy Hopes, and crown thy Joys,
' See how the Fiends with loud and dismal Noise,
' (Presaging Vultures, greedy of their Prey)
' On *Richard*'s Tent their scaly Wings display.
The holy King then offer'd to his View
A lively Tree, on which three Branches grew:
But when the hope of Fruit had made him glad,
All fell to Dust: At which the Earl was sad;
Yet Comfort comes again, when from the Root
He sees a Bough into the North to shoot,
Which nourisht there, extends it self from thence,
And girds this Island with a firm Defence:
There he beholds a high and glorious Throne,
Where sits a King by Laurel Garlands known,
Like bright *Apollo* in the *Muses* Quires,
His radiant Eyes are watchful Heavenly Fires,
Beneath his Feet pale Envy bites her Chain,
And snaky Discord whets her Sting in vain.
' Thou seest (*said* Henry) wise and potent *James*,
' This, this is he, whose happy Union tames
' The savage Feuds, and shall those Lets deface,
' Which keep the Bord'rers from a dear Embrace;
' Both Nations shall in *Britain*'s Royal Crown,
' Their diff'ring Names, the Signs of Faction drown;
' The Silver Streams which from this Spring increase,
' Bedew all Christian's Hearts with Drops of Peace;
' Observe how hopeful *Charles* is born t' asswage
' The Winds, that would disturb this Golden Age.
' When that great King shall full of Glory leave
' The Earth as base, then may this Prince receive
' The Diadem, without his Father's wrong,
' May take it late, and may possess it long;
' Above all *Europe*'s Princes shine thou bright,
' O God's selected Care, and Man's Delight.

Here

Here gentle Sleep forfook his clouded Brows,
And full of holy Thoughts and pious Vows,
He kift the Ground as foon as he arofe,
When watchful *Digby*, who among his Foes
Had wander'd unfufpected all the Night,
Reports that *Richard* is prepar'd to fight.

Long fince the *King* had thought it time to fend
For trufty *Norfolk*, his undaunted Friend,
Who hafting from the Place of his abode,
Found at the Door, a World of Papers ftrow'd;
Some would affright him from the Tyrant's Aid,
Affirming that his Mafter was betray'd;
Some laid before him all thofe bloody Deeds,
From which a Line of fharp Revenge proceeds
With much Compaffion, that fo brave a Knight
Should ferve a Lord, againft whom Angels fight,
And others put Sufpicions in his Mind,
That *Richard* moft obferv'd, was moft unkind.
The *Duke* a while thefe cautious Words revolves
With ferious Thoughts, and thus at laft refolves;
' If all the Camp prove Traytors to my Lord,
' Shall fpotlefs *Norfolk* falfifie his word;
' Mine Oath is paft, I fwore t' uphold his Crown,
' And that fhall fwim, or I with it will drown.
' It is too late now to difpute the Right;
' Dare any Tongue, fince *York* fpread forth his Light,
' *Northumberland*, or *Buckingham* defame,
' Two valiant *Cliffords*, *Roos*, or *Beaumont*'s Name,
' Becaufe they in the weaker Quarrel die?
' They had the *King* with them, and fo have I.
' But ev'ry Eye the Face of *Richard* fhuns,
' For that foul Murder of his Brother's Sons:
' Yet Laws of Knighthood gave me not a Sword
' To ftrike at him, whom all with joynt accord
' Have made my Prince, to whom I Tribute bring:
' I hate his Vices, but adore the King.

' Victorious

' Victorious *Edward,* if thy Soul can hear
' Thy Servant *Howard,* I devoutly swear,
' That to have sav'd thy Children from that Day,
' My hopes on Earth should willingly decay;
' Would *Gloucester* then, my perfect Faith had tried,
' And made two Graves, when noble *Hastings* died.
This said, his Troops he into Order draws,
Then doubled haste redeems his former pause:
So stops the Sailor for a Voyage bound,
When on the Sea he hears the Tempests sound,
Till pressing Hunger to Remembrance sends,
That on his course his Houshold's Life depends:
With this he clears the Doubts that vext his Mind,
And puts his Ship to Mercy of the Wind.

The *Duke's* stout Presence and courageous Looks,
Were to the King as falls of sliding Brooks,
Which bring a gentle and delightful Rest
To weary Eyes, with grievous Care opprest:
He bids that *Norfolk* and his hopeful Son,
(Whose rising Fame in Arms this Day begun)
Should lead the Vantguard: for so great Command,
He dares not trust, in any other hand;
The rest he to his own Advice refers,
And as the Spirit, in that Body stirs,
Then putting on his Crown, a Fatal Sign,
(So offer'd Beasts near Death in Garlands shine,)
He rides about the Ranks, and strives t' inspire
Each Breast with part of his unwearied Fire,
To those who had his Brother's Servants been,
And had the Wonders of his Valour seen,
He saith, ' My Fellow Soldiers, though your Swords
' Are sharp, and need not whetting by my words;
' Yet call to mind those many glorious Days,
' In which we treasur'd up immortal Praise,
' If when I serv'd, I ever fled from Foe,
' Fly ye from mine, let me be punisht so:

' But

' But if my Father, when at firſt he try'd,
' How all his Sons, could ſhining Blades abide,
' Found me an Eagle, whoſe undazled Eyes
' Affront the Beams, which from the Steel ariſe,
' And if I now in Action, teach the ſame,
' Know then, ye have but chang'd your Gen'ral's Name,
' Be ſtill your ſelves, ye fight againſt the Droſs
' Of thoſe, that oft have run from you with Loſs:
' How many *Somerſets*, Diſſentions brands
' Have felt the Force of our revengeful hands?
' From whom this Youth, as from a Princely Flood,
' Derives his beſt, yet not untainted Blood;
' Have our Aſſaults made *Lancaſter* to droop?
' And ſhall the *Welſhman* with his ragged Troop,
' Subdue the *Norman*, and the *Saxon* Line,
' That only *Merlin* may be thought Divine?
' See what a Guide theſe Fugitives have choſe,
' Who bred among the *French* our ancient Foes,
' Forgets the *Engliſh* Language, and the Ground,
' And knows not what our Drums and Trumpets ſound,
To others Minds their willing Oaths he draws,
He tells his juſt Decrees, and healthful Laws,
And makes large Proffers of his future Grace.
Thus having ended, with as chearful Face,
As Nature, which his Step-dame ſtill was thought,
Could lend to one, without Proportion wrought,
Some with loud ſhouting, make the Vallies ring,
But moſt with murmur ſigh: *God ſave the King.*

Now careful *Henry* ſends his Servant *Bray*
To *Stanley*, who accounts it ſafe to ſtay,
And dares not promiſe, leſt his haſte ſhould bring
His Son to Death, now Priſ'nor with the *King*.
About the ſame time *Brakenbury* came,
And thus, to *Stanley* ſaith, in *Richard's* Name,
' My Lord, the King ſalutes you, and commands
' That to his aid, you bring your ready Bands,

' Or

' Or elfe he fwears by him that fits on high,
' Before the Armies joyn, your foon fhall die.
At this the Lord ftood like a Man that hears
The Judge's Voice, which Condemnation bears
Till gath'ring up his Spirits, he replies·
' My Fellow *Haftings* Death hath made me wife,
' More than my Dream could him, for I no more
' Will truft the Tufhes of the angry Boar;
' If with my *George*'s Blood he ftain his Throne,
' I thank my God, I have more Sons than one: '
' Yet to fecure his Life, I quiet ftand
' Againft the King, not lifting up my hand.
The Meffenger departs of hope deny'd.
Then noble *Stanley*, taking *Bray* afide,
Saith: ' Let my Son proceed, without Defpair
' Affifted by his Mother's Alms, and Prayer,
' God will direct both him, and me to take
' Beft Courfes, for that bleffed Woman's fake.
The Earl by this delay, was not inclin'd
To Fear nor Anger, knowing *Stanley*'s Mind,
But calling all his chief Commanders near,
He boldly fpeaks, while they attentive hear.
' It is in vain, brave Friends, to fhew the right
' Which we are forc'd to feek by civil Fight.
' Your Swords are brandifht in a noble Caufe,
' To free your Country from a Tyrant's Jaws.
' What angry Planet? What difaftr'ous Sign
' Directs *Plantagenet*'s afflicted Line?
' Ah! was it not enough, that mutual Rage
' In deadly Battels fhould this Race engage,
' Till by their Blows themfelves they fewer make,
' And Pillars fall, which *France* could never fhake?
' But muft this crooked Monfter now be found,
' To lay rough hands on that unclofed Wound?
' His fecret Plots have much increas'd the Flood,
' He with his Brothers and his Nephews Blood,
' Hath ftain'd the Brightnefs of his Father's Flow'rs,
' And made his own white Rofe as red as ours.

' This

' This is the Day, whofe Splendour puts to flight
' Obfcuring Clouds, and brings an Age of Light.
' We fee no hindrance of thofe wifhed times,
' But this Ufurper, whofe depreffing Crimes
' Will drive him from the Mountain where he ftands,
' So that he needs muft fall without our hands.
' In this we happy are, that by our Arms,
' Both *York* and *Lancafter* revenge their harms.
' Here *Henry*'s Servants joyn, with *Edward*'s Friends,
' And leave their private Griefs for publick Ends.
Thus ceafing, he implores th' Almighty's Grace,
And bids, that every Captain take his place.
His Speech was anfwer'd with a gen'ral Noife
Of Acclamations, doubtlefs figns of Joys
Which Soldiers utter'd as they forward went,
The fure Forerunners of a fair Event;
So when the Winter to the Spring bequeaths
The Rule of Time, and mild *Favonius* breathes,
A Choir of Swans to that fweet Mufick fings,
The Air refounds the Motion of their Wings;
When over Plains they fly in order'd Ranks,
To fport themfelves upon *Cayfters* Banks,

Bold *Oxford* leads the Vantguard up amain,
Whofe valiant Offers heretofore were vain,
When he his Love to *Lancafter* expreft,
But now, with more indulgent Fortune bleft,
His Men he toward *Norfolk*'s Quarter drew,
And ftraight the one the others Enfigns knew,
For they in fev'ral Armies were difplay'd,
This oft in *Edward*'s, that in *Henry*'s Aid:
The fad Remembrance of thofe bloody Fights,
Incens'd new Anger in thefe Noble Knights,
A Marfh lay between, which *Oxford* leaves
Upon his right hand, and the Sun receives
Behind him, with Advantage of the place,
For *Norfolk* muft endure it on his Face,

Ard

And yet his Men advance their Spears and Swords,
Against this Succour, which the Heav'n affords,
His Horse and Foot possest the Field in length,
While Bow-men went before them for their Strength :
Thus marching forth, they set on *Oxford*'s Band,
He fears their Number, and with strict Command,
His Soldiers closely to the Standard draws :
Then *Howard*'s Troops amaz'd begin to pause,
They doubt the Slights of Battel, and prepare
To guard their Valour with a Trench of Care.
This sudden stop made Warlike *Vere* more bold,
To see their Fury in a moment cold ;
His Ranks he in a larger Form displays
Which all were Archers counted in those Days,
The best of *English* Soldiers for their Skill,
Could guide their Shafts according to their Will,
The feather'd Wood they from their Bows let flie,
No Arrow fell, but caus'd some Man to die :
So painful Bees with forward Gladness strive,
To joyn themselves in Throngs before the Hive,
And with Obedience till that Hour attend,
When their Commander shall his watch Word send .
Then to the Winds their tender Sails they yield,
Depress the Flowers depopulate the Field :
Wise *Norfolk* to avoid these Shafts the more,
Contrives his Battel thin and sharp before,
He thus attempts to pierce into the Heart,
And break the Orders of the adverse part,
As when the Cranes direct their Flight on high,
To cut their way, they in a Trigon fly,
Which pointed Figure may with ease divide
Opposing Blast, through which they swiftly glide.

But now the Wings make haste to *Oxford*'s Aid,
The Left by valiant *Savage* was display'd,
His lusty Soldiers were attir'd in White,
They move like Drifts of Snow, whose sudden Fright

Constrains

Conſtrains the weary Paſſenger to ſtay,
And beating on his Face confounds the way.
Brave *Talbot* led the Right, whoſe Grandſire's Name
Was his continual Spur to purchaſe Fame:
Both theſe ruſh'd in, while *Norfolk* like a Wall,
Which oft with Engines crack'd diſdains to fall,
Maintains his Station by defenſive Fight,
Till *Surrey* preſſing forth, with Youthful Might,
Sends many Shadows to the Gates of Death.
When dying Mouths had gaſp'd forth Purple Breath,
His Father follows: Age and former Pains
Had made him ſlower, yet he ſtill retains
His ancient Vigour; and with much Delight
To ſee his Son do Marvels in his ſight,
He ſeconds him, and from the Branches cleaves
Thoſe Cluſters which the former Vintage leaves;
Now *Oxford* flies (as Lightning) through his Troops,
And with his Preſence chears the part that droops .
His brave Endeavours *Surrey*'s Force reſtrain
Like Banks, at which the Ocean ſtorms in vain.
The Swords and Armours ſhine as ſparkling Coals,
Their claſhing drowns the Groans of parting Souls;
The peaceful Neighbours, who had long deſir'd
To find the Cauſes of their Fear expir'd,
Are newly griev'd to ſee this Scarlet Flood,
And *Engliſh* Ground bedew'd with *Engliſh* Blood.
Stout *Rice* and *Herbert* lead the Power of *Wales*,
Their Zeal to *Henry* moves the Hills and Dales
To ſound their Country-man's beloved Name,
Who ſhall reſtore the *Britiſh* Off-ſprings Fame;
Theſe make ſuch Slaughter with their Glaves and Hooks,
That careful *Bards* may fill their precious Books
With Praiſes, which from Warlike Actions ſpring,
And take new Themes, when to their Harps they ſing.
Beſides theſe Soldiers born within this Iſle,
We muſt not of their part the *French* beguile,
Whom *Charles* for *Henry*'s Succour did provide
A Lord of *Scotland*, *Bernard* was their Guide,

A Bloſſom

A Bloſſom of the *Stuarts* happy Line,
Which is on *Britain*'s Throne ordain'd to ſhine :
The Sun, whoſe Rays the Heav'n with Beauty crown,
From his aſcending to his going down,
Saw not a braver Leader in that Age;
And *Boſworth-Field* muſt be the glorious Stage,
In which this *Northern Eagle* learns to flie,
And tries thoſe Wings which after raiſe him high,
When he beyond the ſnowy *Alpes* renown'd,
Shall plant *French Lillies* in *Italian* Ground ;
And cauſe the craggy *Apennine* to know
What Fruits on *Caledonian* Mountains grow.
Now in this Civil War the Troops of *France*,
Their Banners dare on *Engliſh* Air advance,
And on their Launces Points Deſtruction bring
To fainting Servants of the guilty King ;
When heretofore they had no Power to ſtand
Againſt our Armies in their Native Land,
But melting fled, as Wax before the Flame,
Diſmay'd with Thunder of *St. George*'s Name.

Now *Henry* with his Uncle *Pembroke* moves
The Rearward on, and *Stanley* then approves
His Love to *Richmond*'s Perſon, and his Cauſe
He from his Army of three thouſand draws
A few choice Men, and bids the reſt obey
His valiant Brother, who ſhall prove this Day
As famous as great *Warwick*, in whoſe hand
The Fate of *England*'s Crown was thought to ſtand .
With theſe he cloſely ſteals to help his Friend,
While his main Forces ſtir not, but attend
The Younger *Stanley*, and to *Richard*'s Eye
Appear not Parties, but as Standers by.
Yet *Stanley*'s words ſo much the King incenſe
That he exclaims: ' This is a falſe Pretence :
' His doubtful Anſwer ſhall not ſave his Son,
' Young *Strange* ſhall die : See, *Catesby*, this be done.

Now like a Lamb, which taken from the Folds,
The Slaughter-man with rude Embraces holds,
And for his Throat prepares a whetted Knife;
So goes this harmless Lord to end his Life,
The Ax is sharpen'd and the Block prepar'd,
But worthy *Ferrers* equal Portion shar'd,
Of Grief and Terror which the Pris'ner felt,
His tender Eyes in Tears of Pity melt,
And hasting to the King he boldly said;
' My Lord, too many bloody Stains are laid
' By envious Tongues upon your peaceful Reign;
' O may their Malice ever speak in vain:
' Afford not this advantage to their Spite,
' None should be kill'd to day, but in the Fight:
' Your Crown is strongly fix'd, your Cause is good;
' Cast not upon it Drops of harmless Blood;
' His Life is nothing, yet will dearly cost,
' If while you seek it, we perhaps have lost
' Occasions of your Conquest thither flie,
' Where Rebels arm'd, with cursed Blades shall die,
' And yield in Death to your victorious Awe:
' Let naked hands be censur'd by the Law.
Such Pow'r his Speech and seemly Action hath,
It mollifies the Tyrant's bloody Wrath,
And he commands that *Strange*'s Death be stay'd.
The Noble Youth (who was before dismay'd
At Death's approaching sight) now sweetly clears
His cloudy Sorrows, and forgets his Fears.
As when a Steer to burning Altars led,
Expecting fatal Blows to cleave his Head,
Is by the Priest for some Religious Cause
Sent back to live, and now in Quiet draws
The open Air, and takes his wonted Food,
And never thinks how near to Death he stood:

The King, though ready, yet his March delay'd,
To have *Northumberland*'s expected Aid.

To

To him, induſtrious *Ratcliffe* ſwiftly hies;
But *Percy* greets him thus · ‘ My troubled Eyes
‘ This Night beheld my Father's angry Ghoſt,
‘ Adviſing not to joyn with *Richard*'s Hoſt:
‘ Wilt thou (*ſaid he*) ſo much obſcure my Shield,
‘ To bear mine Azure Lion in the Field
‘ With ſuch a Gen'ral? Ask him, on which ſide
‘ His Sword was drawn when I at *Towton* died.
When *Richard* knew that both his hopes were vain,
He forward ſets with Curſing and Diſdain,
And cries: ‘ Who would not all theſe Lords deteſt?
‘ When *Percy* changeth, like the Moon his Creſt.
This Speech the Heart of Noble *Ferrers* rent:
He anſwers: ‘ Sir, though many dare repent,
‘ That which they cannot now without your wrong,
‘ And only grieve they have been true too long,
‘ My Breaſt ſhall never bear ſo foul a Stain,
‘ If any ancient Blood in me remain,
‘ Which from the *Norman* Conqu'rors took Deſcent,
‘ It ſhall be wholly in your Service ſpent;
‘ I will obtain to day alive or dead,
‘ The Crowns that grace a faithful Soldier's Head.
‘ Bleſt be thy tongue (*replies the King*) in thee,
‘ The Strength of all thine Anceſtors I ſee,
‘ Extending Warlike Arms for *England*'s Good,
‘ By thee their Heir, in Valour as in Blood.

But here we leave the King, and muſt review
Thoſe Sons of *Mars*, who cruel Blades imbrue
In Rivers ſprung from Hearts that Bloodleſs lie,
And ſtain their ſhining Arms in ſanguine Dye.
Here valiant *Oxford* and fierce *Norfolk* meet,
And with their Spears each other rudely greet;
About the Air the ſhiver'd Pieces play,
Then on their Swords their Noble Hands they lay,
And *Norfolk* firſt a Blow directly guides
To *Oxford*'s Head, which from his Helmet ſlides

Upon

Upon his Arm, and biting through the Steel,
Inflicts a Wound, which *Vere* difdains to feel,
He lifts his Fauchion with a threatning Grace,
And hews the Bever off from *Howard*'s Face.
This being done, he with Compaffion charm'd,
Retires, afham'd to ftrike a Man difarm'd :
But ftraight a deadly Shaft fent from a Bow,
(Whofe Mafter, though far off, the Duke could know
Untimely brought this Combat to an end,
And pierc'd the Brain of *Richard*'s conftant Friend.
When *Oxford* faw him fink, his Noble Soul
Was full of Grief, which made him thus condole :
' Farewel, true Knight, to whom no coftly Grave
' Can give due Honour : Would my Tears might fave
' Thofe Streams of Blood, deferving to be fpilt
' In better Service : Had not *Richard*'s Guilt
' Such heavy Weight upon his Fortune laid,
' Thy glorious Vertues had his Sins outweigh'd,
Courageous *Talbot* had with *Surrey* met,
And after many Blows begins to fret,
That one fo young in Arms fhould thus unmov'd,
Refift his Strength, fo oft in War approv'd.
And now the Earl beholds his Father fall ;
Whofe Death like horrid Darknefs frighted all :
Some give themfelves as Captives, others flie,
But this young Lion cafts his gen'rous Eye
On *Mowbrayes* Lion, painted in his Shield,
And with that King of Beafts repines to yield :
' The Field (*faith he*) in which the Lion ftands,
' Is Blood, and Blood I offer to the hands
' Of daring Foes ; but never fhall my Flight
' Die black my Lion, which as yet is white.
His Enemies (like cunning Huntfmen) ftrive
In binding Snares, to take their Prey alive,
While he defires t' expofe his naked Breaft,
And thinks the Sword that deepeft ftrikes is beft.
Young *Howard* fingle with an Army fights,
When mov'd with Pity two Renowned Knights,

Strong *Clarindon*, and valiant *Coniers* trie
To rescue him, in which attempt they die ;
For *Savage* red with Blood of slaughter'd Foes,
Doth them in midst of all his Troops inclose,
Where though the Captain for their Safety strives,
Yet baser hands deprive them of their Lives.
Now *Surrey* fainting, scarce his Sword can hold,
Which made a common Soldier grow so bold,
To lay rude hands upon that Noble Flower ;
Which he disdaining (Anger gives him Power)
Erects his Weapon with a nimble round,
And sends the Peasants Arm to kiss the Ground.
This done, to *Talbot* he presents his Blade,
And saith, ' It is not hope of Life hath made
' This my Submission, but my Strength is spent,
' And some perhaps of Villain Blood will vent
' My weary Soul: This Favour I demand,
' That I may die by your victorious hand.
' Nay, God forbid that any of my Name,
' (*Quoth* Talbot) should put out so bright a Flame,
' As burns in thee (brave Youth) where thou hast err'd,
' It was thy Father's fault, since he preferr'd
' A Tyrant's Crown before the juster Side.
The Earl still mindful of his Birth replied,
' I wonder (*Talbot*) that thy Noble Heart
' Insults on Ruines of the vanquisht part :
' We had the right, if now to you it flow,
' The Fortune of your Swords hath made it so :
' I never will my luckless Choice repent,
' Nor can it stain mine Honour or Descent,
' Set *England's* Royal Wreath upon a *Stake*,
' There will I fight, and not the place forsake :
' And if the Will of God hath so dispos'd,
' That *Richmond's* Brow be with the Crown inclos'd,
' I shall to him, or his give doubtless Sighs,
' That Duty in my Thoughts, not Faction, shines.
The earnest Soldiers still the Chase pursue :
But their Commanders grieve they should imbrue

Their

Their Swords in Blood which springs from *English* Veins,
The peaceful Sound of Trumpets then restrains
From further Slaughter, with a mild Retreat
To rest contented in this first Defeat.

The King intended at his setting out,
To help his Vantguard, but a nimble Scout
Runs crying; ' *Sir*, I saw not far from hence,
' Where *Richmond* hovers with a small Defence,
' And like one guilty of some heinous Ill,
' Is cover'd with the Shade of yonder Hill.
The Raven almost famish'd joys not more,
When restless Billows tumble to the Shore
A heap of Bodies shipwrack'd in the Seas,
Than *Richard* with this News himself doth please:
He now diverts his Course another way,
And with his Army led in fair Array,
Ascends the rising Ground, and taking view
Of *Henry's* Soldiers, sees they are but few :
Imperial Courage fires his Noblest Breast,
He sets a threat'ning Spear within his rest,
Thus saying; ' All true Knights, on me attend;
' I soon will bring this Quarrel to an end :
' If none will follow, if all Faith be gone,
' Behold, I go to try my Cause alone ;
He strikes his Spurs into his Horse's side,
With him stout *Lovell* and bold *Ferrers* ride;
To them brave *Ratcliffe*; gen'rous *Clifton* haste,
Old *Brakenbury* scorns to be the last :
As born with Wings, all worthy Spirits flie,
Resolv'd for Safety of their Prince to die ;
And *Catesby* to this Number adds his Name,
Though pale with Fear, yet overcome with Shame:
Their Boldness *Richmond* dreads not, but admires;
He sees their Motion like to rolling Fires,
Which by the Wind along the Fields are born
Amidst the Trees, the Hedges, and the Corn,

C   Where

Where they the hopes of Husbandmen confume,
And fill the troubled Air with dusky Fume.
Now as a careful Lord of Neighb'ring Grounds,
He keeps the Flame from entring in his Bounds,
Each Man is warn'd to hold his Station fure,
Prepar'd with Courage strong Affaults t'endure :
But all in vain, no Force, no Warlike Art,
From fudden breaking can preferve that part,
Where *Richard* like a Dart from Thunder falls :
His Foes give way, and stand as brazen Walls
On either fide of his inforced Path,
While he neglects them, and referves hi Wrath
For him whofe Death thefe threat'ning Clouds would clear,
Whom now with Gladnefs he beholdeth near,
And all thofe Faculties together brings,
Which move the Soul to high and noble things.
Ev'n fo a Tyger having follow'd long
The Hunter's steps that robb'd her of her Young :
When first she fees him, is by Rage inclin'd
Her steps to double, and her Teeth to grind.

Now Horfe to Horfe, and Man is joyn'd to Man
So strictly, that the Soldiers hardly can
Their Adverfaries from their Fellows know :
Here each brave Champion fingles out his Foe.
In this Confufion *Brakenbury* meets
With *Hungerford*, and him thus foully greets :
' Ah Traytor, falfe in Breach of Faith and Love,
' What Difcontent could thee and *Bourchier* move,
' Who had fo long my Fellows been in Arms,
' To flie to Rebels ? What feducing Charms
' Could on your clouded Minds fuch Darknefs bring,
' To ferve an Out-Law, and neglect the King ?
With thefe fharp Speeches *Hungerford* enrag'd,
T'uphold his Honour, thus the Battel wag'd :
' Thy doting Age (*faith he*) delights in words,
' But this Afperfion muft be try'd by Swords,

Then

Then leaving Talk, he by his Weapon speaks,
And drives a Blow, which *Brackenbury* breaks
By lifting up his Left Hand, else the Steel
Had pierc'd his Burgonet, and made him feel
The Pangs of Death : But now the Fury fell
Upon the Hand that did the Stroke repel,
And cuts so large a Portion of the Shield,
That it no more can safe Protection yield.
Bold *Hungerford* disdains his Use to make
Of this advantage, but doth straight forsake
His massy Target, render'd to his 'Squire,
And saith : ' Let Cowards such Defence desire.
This done, these valiant Knights dispose their Blades,
And still the one the other's Face invades,
Till *Brakenbury's* Helmet giving way
To those fierce Strokes that *Hungerford* doth lay,
Is bruis'd and gapes, which *Bourchier* fighting near,
Perceives and cries : ' Brave *Hungerford* forbear,
' Bring not those Silver Hairs to timeless end,
' He was, and may be once again our Friend.
But oh, too late ! the fatal Blow was sent
From *Hungerford*, which he may now repent,
But not recal, and digs a Mortal Wound
In *Brakenbury's* Head, which should be crown'd
With precious Metals, and with Bays adorn'd
For constant Truth appearing, when he scorn'd
To stain his hand in those young Princes Blood,
And like a Rock amidst the Ocean stood
Against the Tyrant's Charms, and Threats unmov'd,
Though Death declares how much he *Richard* lov'd.
Stout *Ferrers* strives to fix his mighty Launce
In *Pembroke's* Heart, which on the Steel doth glance,
And runs in vain the empty Air to press :
But *Pembroke's* Spear obtaining wisht Success,
Through *Ferrers* Breast-plate and his Body sinks,
And Vital Blood from inward Vessels drinks.
Here *Stanley* and brave *Lovell* try their Strength,
Whose equal Courage draws the Strife to length,

They

They think not how they may themselves defend,
To strike is all their Care, to kill, their end.
So meet two Bulls upon adjoyning Hills
Of Rocky *Charnwood*, while their Murmur fills
The hollow Crag, when striving for their Bounds,
They wash their piercing Horns in mutual Wounds.

If in the midst of such a bloody Fight
The Name of Friendship be not thought too light,
Recount my Muse, how *Byron*'s faithful Love
To dying *Clifton* did it self approve:
For *Clifton* fighting bravely in the Troop,
Receives a Wound, and now begins to droop:
Which *Byron* seeing, though in Arms his Foe,
In Heart his Friend, and hoping that the Blow
Had not been mortal, guards him with his Shield
From second Hurts, and cries, ' Dear *Clifton*, yield,
' Thou hither cam'st led by sinister Fate,
' Against my first Advice, yet now, though late,
' Take this my Counsel. *Clifton* thus replied :
' It is too late, for I must now provide
' To seek another Life: Live thou, sweet Friend,
' And when thy side obtains a happy end,
' Upon the Fortunes of my Children look,
' Remember what a solemn Oath he took,
' That he whose part should prove the best in Fight,
' Would with the Conqu'ror try his utmost Might,
' To save the other Lands from rav'nous Paws,
' Which seize on Fragments of a luckless Cause.
' My Father's Fall our House had almost drown'd,
' But I by chance aboard in Shipwreck found.
' May never more such Danger threaten mine.
' Deal thou for them, as I would do for thine.
This said, his Senses fail, and Pow'rs decay,
While *Byron* calls, 'Stay, worthy *Clifton*, stay,
' And hear my faithful Promise once again,
' Which if I break, may all my Deeds be vain.

But now he knows that Vital Breath is fled,
And needless words are utter'd to the dead ;
Into the midst of *Richard*'s Strength he flies,
Presenting glorious Acts to *Henry*'s Eyes,
And for his Service he expects no more,
Than *Clifton*'s Son from Forfeits to restore.

While *Richard* bearing down with eager Mind,
The Steps by which his Passage was confin'd,
Lays hands on *Henry*'s Standard as his Prey ;
Strong *Brandon* bore it, whom this fatal Day
Marks with a black Note, as the only Knight,
That on the conqu'ring part forsakes the Light.
But Time, whose Wheels with various Motion run,
Repays this Service fully to his Son,
Who marries *Richmond*'s Daughter, born between
Two Royal Parents, and endowed a Queen.
When now the King perceives that *Brandon* strives
To save his Charge, he sends a Blow that rives
His Skull in twain, and by a gaping Hole,
Gives ample Scope to his departing Soul,
And thus insults ; ' Accursed Wretch, farewel,
' Thine Ensigns now may be display'd in Hell :
' There thou shalt know it is an odious thing,
' To let thy Banner fly against thy King.
With Scorn he throws the Standard to the Ground,
When *Cheney* for his Height and Strength renown'd,
Steps forth to cover *Richmond*, now expos'd
To *Richard*'s Sword : The King with *Cheney* clos'd,
And to the Earth this mighty Giant fell'd.
Then like a Stag, whom Fences long with-held
From Meadows, where the Spring in Glory reigns,
Now having levell'd those unpleasing Chains,
And treading proudly on the vanquisht Flowers,
He in his Hopes a thousand Joys devours :
For now no Pow'r to cross his end remains,
But only *Henry*, whom he never dains

To name his Foe, and thinks he shall not brave
A valiant Champion, but a yielding Slave.
Alas! How much deceiv'd, when he shall find
An able Body and courageous Mind:
For *Richmond* boldly doth himself oppose
Against the King, and gives him Blows for Blows,
Who now confesseth with an angry Frown
His Rival, not unworthy of the Crown.

The Younger *Stanley* then no longer staid,
The Earl in Danger needs his present Aid,
Which he performs as sudden as the Light,
His coming turns the Ballance of the Fight.
So threat'ning Clouds, whose Fall the Plow-men fear,
Which long upon the Mountains top appear,
Dissolve at last, and Vapours then distil
To wat'ry Showers that all the Vallies fill.
The first that saw this dreadful Storm arise,
Was *Catesby*, who to *Richard* loudly cries,
' No way but swift Retreat your Life to save,
' It is no Shame with Wings t' avoid the Grave.
This said, he trembling turns himself to fly,
And dares not stay to hear the King's Reply,
Who scorning his Advice, as foul and base,
Returns this Answer with a wrathful Face;
' Let Cowards trust their Horses nimble Feet,
' And in their course with new Destruction meet,
' Gain thou some Hours to draw thy fearful Breath:
' To me ignoble Flight is worse than Death.
But at th' approach of *Stanley*'s fresh Supply,
The King's side droops: so gen'rous Horses lie
Unapt to stir, or make their Courage known,
Which under cruel Masters sink and groan.
There at his Prince's Foot stout *Ratcliffe* dies,
Not fearing, but despairing, *Lovell* flies;
For he shall after end his weary Life
In not so fair, but yet as bold a Strife.

The

The King maintains the Fight, though left alone :
For *Henry's* Life he fain would change his own,
And as a *Lioness*, which compass'd round
With Troops of Men, receives a smarting Wound
By some bold hand, though hinder'd and opprest
With other Spears, yet slighting all the rest,
Will follow him alone that wrong'd her first :
So *Richard* pressing with revengeful Thirst,
Admits no Shape but *Richmond's* to his Eye,
And would in triumph on his Carcase die :
But that great God, to whom all Creatures yield,
Protects his Servant with a Heav'nly Shield,
His Pow'r in which the Earl securely trusts,
Rebates the Blows, and falsifies the Thrusts.
The King grows weary, and begins to faint,
It grieves him that his Foes perceive the taint :
Some strike him, that till then durst not come near,
With Weight and Number they to Ground him bear,
Where trampled down, and hew'd with many Swords,
He softly utter'd these his dying Words,
' Now Strength no longer Fortune can withstand,
' I perish in the Center of my Land.
His hand he then with Wreaths of Grass infolds,
And bites the Earth which he so strictly holds,
As if he would have born it with him hence,
So loth he was to lose his Right's Pretence.

FINIS.

A Catalogue of Poems, &c. *Printed and Sold by* H. Hills, *in* Black-Fryars, *near the* Water-fide; *where feveral more may be had that are not here Inferted.*

A Congratulatory Poem on Prince *George* of *Denmark*, &c. on the Succefs at Sea

Marlborough Still Conquers

The Flight of the Pretender.

Honefty in Diftrefs, a Tragedy.

The Kit Cats a Poem, &c

Wine, a Poem, &c

Cyder, a Poem, in 2 Books, with the Splendid Shilling, &c

The Pleafures of a Single Life, &c.

Faction Difplay'd

Moderation Difplay'd

The Duel of the Stags. &c

Coopers-Hill, by Sir *J* Denham

An Effay on Poetry, by the Earl of *Mulgrave*

Abfalom and *Achitophel.*

The Plague of *Athens*

A Satyr againft Man and Woman

The Forgiving Husband

Inftructions to *Vanderbank*

The Temple of Death

An Effay on Tranflated Verfe, by the Earl of *Rofcomon*

Horace Or the Art of Poetry

The Hiftory of Infipids

The Swan Trip Club

Lucretius on Death, &c

The Medal againft Sedition.

Bellizarius a great Commander

Daphnis, or a Paftoral Elegy &c

A Poem on the Countefs of *Abingdon.*

Nundinæ Sturbrigienfes,

Tunbrigialia

An Ode on the Incarnation, &c.

Hoglandiæ Defcriptio.

Milton's Sublimity on Cyder

Bofworth fei'ld, a Poem, by Sir *John Beaumount* Bar

Milton's Sublimity afferted, in anfwer to Cyder, a Poem

Canary Birds Naturaliz'd

Baucis and *Philemon*, &c

Circus, a Satyr. Or the Ring in Hide Park

St *James's* Park, a Satyr

The Spleen, a Pindarique Ode, & *Philips's* Paftorale.

A Letter from *Italy*, to my Lord *Halifax*, with other Poems

Blenheim, a Poem, by *Philips*

Mac Flecknoe, by *J Dryden*, with *Spencer's* Ghoft, by *J Oldham*

The Female Reign, an Ode by *Sam Cobb*

The Upftart, a Satyr

A Poem on the Taking St. *Mary*

Windfor Caftle, a Poem.

The Servitor, a Poem.

The Pulpit War

The Campaign, a Poem, by Mr *Addifon*

The Counter Scuffle, a Poem

Don *Francifco Sutoriofo*

Confolation to *Mira* mourning.

A Panegyrick on *Oliver Cromwel*, with three Poems on his Death

A Poem in Defence of the Church of *England.*

The Apparition, a Poem.

The *Hind* and *Panther* Tranfvos'd to the Story of the Country Moufe and City Moufe.

Dr *Gath's* Difpenfary

The Memoirs on the Right Vilainous *John Hall*, the late Famous and Notorious Robber, &c

Mr *Shaftoe's* Narrative giving an Account of the Birth of the Pretended Prince of *Wale*, &c.

Lightning Source UK Ltd.
Milton Keynes UK
UKHW052003221222
414360UK00014B/121